20038071a6

W9-DFC-290

BACK OFF! ANIMAL DEFENSES
UNDERCOVER ANIMALS

by Nadia Higgins

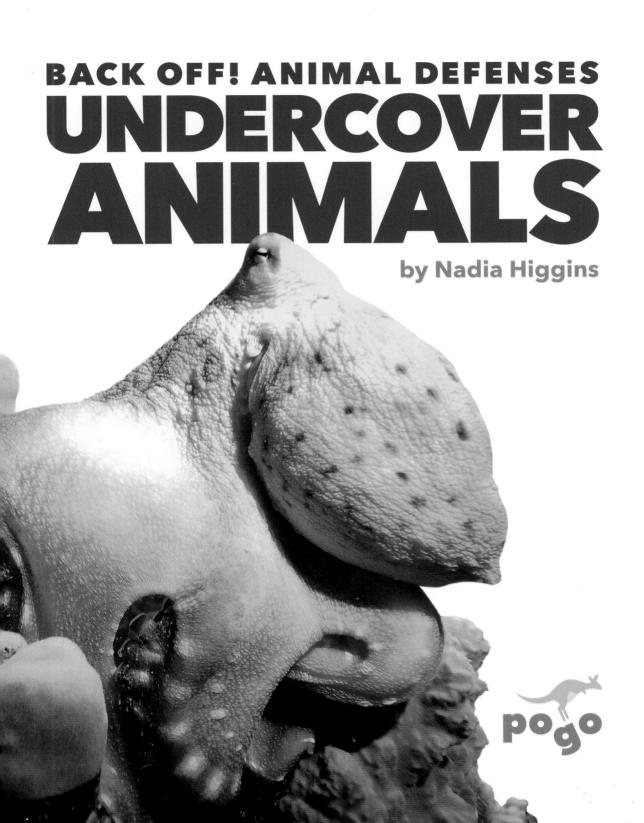

pogo

Ideas for Parents and Teachers

Pogo Books let children practice reading informational text while introducing them to nonfiction features such as headings, labels, sidebars, maps, and diagrams, as well as a table of contents, glossary, and index.

Carefully leveled text with a strong photo match offers early fluent readers the support they need to succeed.

Before Reading

- "Walk" through the book and point out the various nonfiction features. Ask the student what purpose each feature serves.
- Look at the glossary together. Read and discuss the words.

Read the Book

- Have the child read the book independently.
- Invite him or her to list questions that arise from reading.

After Reading

- Discuss the child's questions. Talk about how he or she might find answers to those questions.
- Prompt the child to think more. Ask: Have you seen any of the camouflaged animals mentioned in the book? Can you think of any camouflaged animals that aren't discussed?

Pogo Books are published by Jump!
5357 Penn Avenue South
Minneapolis, MN 55419
www.jumplibrary.com

Library of Congress Cataloging-in-Publication Data

Higgins, Nadia, author.
 Undercover animals / by Nadia Higgins.
   pages cm. – (Back off! Animal defenses)
 Audience: Ages 7-10.
 Summary: "Carefully leveled text and vibrant photographs introduce readers to animals that blend in with their environment, such as the octopus, Arctic hare, silk moth, and zebra, and explore how they use camouflage to defend themselves against predators. Includes activity, glossary, and index."
–Provided by publisher.
 Includes bibliographical references and index.
 ISBN 978-1-62031-307-7 (hardcover: alk. paper) –
 ISBN 978-1-62496-373-5 (ebook)
 1. Camouflage (Biology)–Juvenile literature.
 2. Protective coloration (Biology)–Juvenile literature.
 3. Animal defenses–Juvenile literature. I. Title.
 QL767.H54 2016
 591.47'2–dc23
                                                  2015033310

Series Editor: Jenny Fretland VanVoorst
Series Designer: Anna Peterson
Book Designer: Ellen Schofield
Photo Researcher: Jenny Fretland VanVoorst

Photo Credits: All photos by Shutterstock except: Corbis, 16; Dreamstime, 20-21; Getty, 5; iStock, cover; Nature Picture Library, 17; SuperStock, 4, 8-9, 11.

Printed in the United States of America at Corporate Graphics in North Mankato, Minnesota.

TABLE OF CONTENTS

CHAPTER 1

LOOK AGAIN

In a **rain forest**, a leaf-tailed gecko hangs on a tree trunk. Bright sun beats on the lizard's back. Can you see it? Look again.

The little lizard relies on **camouflage** to stay safe. Its flat body blends in with the tree. Even the markings on its skin look like bark. A hungry snake does not notice it.

How do you blend in when you live in water? A glass catfish has one answer. Its body is see-through, like glass. The colors of the river show through it. Hungry birds fly right on by.

Some camouflage does not seem to make sense. Look at a zebra. Its stripes are so bold. How could they hide anything?

Zebras blend in with each other. They move in a **herd** over a grassland. To a lion, the zebras look like a bunch of crazy stripes. The **predator** does not know where to strike.

CHAPTER 2

COSTUME CHANGES

In the **tundra**, an Arctic hare digs in the snow. Nearby, a fox is on the hunt. It scans the icy land. But its eyes pass over the hare's white fur.

In spring, the snow melts. The land becomes gray. Luckily, the hare changes with the seasons. Its fur becomes gray too.

An octopus senses danger as it glides over the ocean floor. It changes costume faster than a superhero. Flash! It goes from white to gray. Spots appear. Its skin can even add bumps and spikes. The octopus looks like the rocks around it.

DID YOU KNOW?

An octopus is **color-blind**. So how does it know what color to change into? Scientists are trying to figure out that mystery.

Seconds later, the octopus is hiding in a clump of orange seaweed. Its body turns orange. The spots go away. Its skin is as smooth as the plant.

TAKE A LOOK!

Animals blend in through shape, color, and pattern.

SHAPE
An Arabian camel lives among desert hills.
From far away, its hump looks like another hill.

COLOR
A green parrot seems to disappear in a tree.

PATTERN
Forest plants make many long, thin shadows.
A baby tapir's stripes help it blend in.

CHAPTER 3

COPYCATS

Two snakes slither through a pile of leaves. Can you tell them apart? Their stripe patterns are just a little different. But one has a bite that can stop your heart.

eastern coral snake

That is the eastern coral snake. The scarlet kingsnake is a harmless copycat. Even so, predators stay away when they see those stripes.

scarlet kingsnake

In the desert, a **burrowing** owl looks out from its underground nest. Above, a hungry coyote is looking for **prey**.

The coyote comes too close. Hissssss! The little owl sounds just like a rattlesnake. The coyote falls for the trick. It turns away from the sound of danger.

Far away in a forest, a silk moth lands on a tree branch. The giant moth is looking for a **mate**. Nearby, a hungry cat stands ready to pounce.

When the moth flaps its wings, the cat jumps back. It thinks a great horned owl has spotted it. But the owl eyes are just markings on moth's wings. The moth continues its search through the night.

TAKE A LOOK!

These animals are so good at copying they could win a contest!

 ## BEST LEAF IMITATION

This bug's name says it all.
It is called a walking leaf.

 ## BEST POOP COSTUME

This caterpillar looks just like
a bird dropping. It will turn into
a giant swallowtail butterfly.

 ## NO. 1 STUMP

A potoo bird is sitting on a tree stump.
Can you see it?

ACTIVITIES & TOOLS

MAKE YOUR OWN CAMOUFLAGE

Can you camouflage your favorite toy animal? Make a habitat that hides it in plain sight.

You will need:
- a toy animal
- a box that is bigger than your animal
- markers
- construction paper
- scissors
- glue
- rocks, sticks, and leaves from outside (optional)

Steps:

❶ Turn your box into a home for your animal. It should have three sides. You many just have to take off the lid. Or, an adult can help you cut one side off.

❷ The box is like a stage for your animal. Where will your animal stand? Mark its spot with an X.

❸ Think about how you will decorate your box to camouflage your animal. What colors will help your animal blend in? What shapes? What patterns?

❹ Cut out shapes of construction paper. Glue them to your box.

❺ Add more camouflage with markers. Add patterns or drawings. If you want, place leaves, rocks, and sticks from outside.

❻ Put your animal it its spot. Does it blend in? Your animal will be safe in its camouflage.

GLOSSARY

burrowing: Digging in the ground to make a home.

camouflage: The hiding or disguising of something by covering it up or changing the way it looks.

color-blind: Unable to see differences among colors.

herd: A group of animals that live together.

mate: A partner for making babies.

predator: An animal that kills other animals for food.

prey: An animal that is killed and eaten by other animals.

rain forest: A warm, rainy forest with lots of green plants and many kinds of animals.

tundra: Flat, treeless land that is cold and snowy most of the time.

INDEX

TO LEARN MORE

Learning more is as easy as 1, 2, 3.

1) Go to www.factsurfer.com

2) Enter "undercoveranimals" into the search box.

3) Click the "Surf" button to see a list of websites.

With factsurfer, finding more information is just a click away.